Saltwater Fishing

Tackle, Rigging, How & When To Fish

By Jack Zinzow

 Publishing, Inc.

105 NE 25th St.   P.O. Box 371005   Miami, FL 33137

Front cover photos: angler and crew landing blue marlin aboard Sportfisherman, Sandra Romashko; tarpon fishing by seven-mile bridge in Marathon, Florida, and flats fishing in Islamorada, Florida, Monroe County Tourist Development Council. *Back cover:* black marlin, Bill Staros.

Contents

Foreword

It has been my experience that a small percentage of the fishermen catch most of the fish. There are at least two reasons for this. **1.** A small percentage of the fishermen fish many hours a day and many days each year. **2.** An even smaller percentage of the fishermen are willing to prepare themselves and their gear in advance of their fishing trips.

It is from this second group of highy efficient fishermen that we can all learn the most. The fisherman who can fish hundreds of hours each month should catch a lot of fish. However, I really admire the angler who goes out only two or three days a month and always has a hot fishing trip.

Because I am fortunate to live in the best saltwater fishing area in America, I have had an excellent opportunity to meet and fish with skilled and successful saltwater fishermen. This book is a compilation of the best techniques of this select group. I have made a point of observing and trying the methods that the successful saltwater fishermen use, and then compiling notes on the techniques that work.

These are not short cuts. Fishing has this in common with all sports — if you will be good at it, you must make the effort. If you decide the effort is not worthwhile, then don't be surprised when the other guy gets the fish.

The methods covered in this book will allow you to make the largest part of the effort before you leave land and let you spend your time at sea for the reason you're there, catching fish!   —JRZ

First of All

Anyone can enjoy sportfishing: the equipment needed is minimal, but the pleasure is immense. The fisherman can wade the flats for bonefish, permit, or even shark. Fishing from bridges or banks will produce snapper, grunt, and sometimes snook — all delicious on the table. Sportfishing can be exciting on a bass boat in the many bays and rivers of the southeast U.S. coasts and the Gulf of Mexico. And the sportfishing boat can be anything from a well equipped 18-foot open fisherman up to a 50-foot charter boat. Also drift boats, or as they are called in some areas, head boats, are available inexpensively, and all rods, reels, and bait are furnished.

So anyone can be a sportfisherman. In this book all methods of fishing will be discussed. However some applications apply to all types of saltwater angling, regardless what kind of equipment is used.

First and foremost you must know the state game laws and limits, and if you fish offshore, the federal laws as well. Not the captain, not your fellow fishermen, but only you are responsible for playing by the rules. This information is available from the states where you plan to fish, the U.S. Government wildlife services, and most bait and tackle shops. In the past the laws were so simple that a book like this would include them. Today we are trying to preserve the pleasure of fishing for future generations, so the laws change very often.

All anglers must be aware of safety at all times. In the excitement of the moment people do slip off bridges and banks, and waders do step into holes that look like a dark patch of weeds. Anyone offshore can be three hours from medical assistance. Boats do both burn and sink in spite of safe operating practices. Very rarely lightning will strike with devastating results. But there are very few boating *accidents*. Most problems are caused by inadvertence, alcohol or ignorance. If you would enjoy this great and relaxing sport, use your head, avoid storms, don't drink alcohol until you are through cleaning the catch and tied up in port, and carry the basic safety equipment required by the Coast Guard.

One of the real pleasures of fishing is eating the catch. If you or someone you know is not going to eat the fish release it at once, in the best condition possible. However if the fish is to be kept, be certain it is adequately iced, or over iced. The surest method of icing the catch is to put it in a cooler with plenty of ice and a bucket or two of salt water. If this is done and you clean the fish within a few hours, the fish will be delicious and healthful when eaten.

A word about ciguatera, a poison which is passed to us by large reef fish. The condition is almost unknown in pelagic fish such as dolphin, wahoo, cobia and billfish, but the dangerous and potentially fatal poison is frequently carried by large groupers and barracudas. Reef fishes are susceptible. If you are a visitor, seek local information regarding the prevalence of ciguatera in that area's fishery.

Fishing Line

Your first decision is what kind of fish you are going to catch. If you are likely to catch fish of 1 to 5 pounds, fishing will be enjoyable sport with a 6- or 8-pound test line. For fish of 6 to 30 pounds consider 10- to 15-pound test line. If you are seeking larger fish, try 20- or 30-pound test line. Notice the word "test".

Fishing lines are classified as either test or class, and the difference is significant. A test line has the manufacturer's assurance that the

Fishing lines come in a variety of colors and spool sizes, as well as a wide range of test or class weights.

line will not break at a steady pull of less than the stated test. A class line is assured to break at the stated class, or even at slightly less weight. Thus frequently a line of 17-pound test is an I.G.F.A. class 30-pound line. (I.G.F.A. are the initials for International Game Fish Association, the worldwide association of interested fishermen that sets the standards and keeps the records of fish caught.) Throughout this book all fishing lines referred to are the test category.

So the process is simple, first decide the weight of fish you are looking for, pick out the proper test line, and then get a balanced rod and reel for that test weight of line. Balance is very important. Fishermen refer to a 6-pound rig, a 12-pound rig and so on. Some manufacturers even name their reels 20, 30, 50, 80, and 130. This directly states the optimum line test weight for that reel. Others use vaguer terms like ultra-light, light, medium, and heavy. Whatever the terms, be certain to match the fish, the lure, the line, the reel and the rod.

The line is the most critical part of any fishing gear. Nicked or frayed line can lose many lures and fish You must change the line when its condition warrants. Some expert anglers change their lines after every fishing day. This is not necessary unless you are after record fish on very light line, or if you had a particularly lengthy fight with a fish. The lighter the line the more easily it is worn to the breaking point. You must inspect the line after every fishing trip. Look carefully for nicks or frays. If you have many flaws, and you haven't been fishing oyster bars, try to find the cause. Most often excessive wear will be traced to rough, missing, or split guides on the rod. Often you can strip off 50 or so yards off the reel and have the benefit of new line without changing the entire spool. But in this situation you will sacrifice the amount of line you have available to fight the fish. Consider buying your line on "service" spools. This not only will save money, it will encourage you to put on new line frequently. Sometimes you will see a fishing boat empty reels by letting the line trail in the water behind a running boat. This is an easy way to empty your reels, but never do it! This practice is extremely destructive of the fishing habitat.

Stripping line off your reel is slightly tedious, but it must be done. Some thought can make the task easier. Using an inexpensive quarter-inch drill in a drill press stand can make the task much faster. Put a dowel rod in the chuck of the drill, tape the end of the line to the dowel and turn on the drill. With a little practice the line will flow off the reel quickly. The line that was in the interior center of the reel is now the outside line on the dowel. This line was probably never off the reel and therefore it is free of flaws, excellent for leaders or rigging bait.

Rods and Reels

If you are a novice fisherman, start by going to a store that specializes in fishing and boating gear. Initially, you will want the aid of a knowledgable salesperson in making your selection. There are five types of saltwater fishing gear: spinning tackle, flycasting tackle, baitcasting tackle, boat tackle, surfcasting tackle.

Discussion of each type of fishing equipment follows. Start your search at a tackle shop; as you gain more experience you can take advantage of the prices and selection offered by the discount stores. Eventually, you may want custom-made gear, either professionally made, or home made. Many anglers make beautiful rods at home, made exactly the way they want the rods to feel and react.

Regardless what kind of tackle is involved, the feel of the rod is very important and must be comfortable.

Spinning Gear

Spinning rods and reels are the easiest to use. Use these rigs to cast with light- to medium-weight lures. The technique is simple—hold the rod in your primary hand (the right hand if you are right handed, or the

Saltwater Fishing Rods

deep sea   surf   spinning   baitcasting   fly

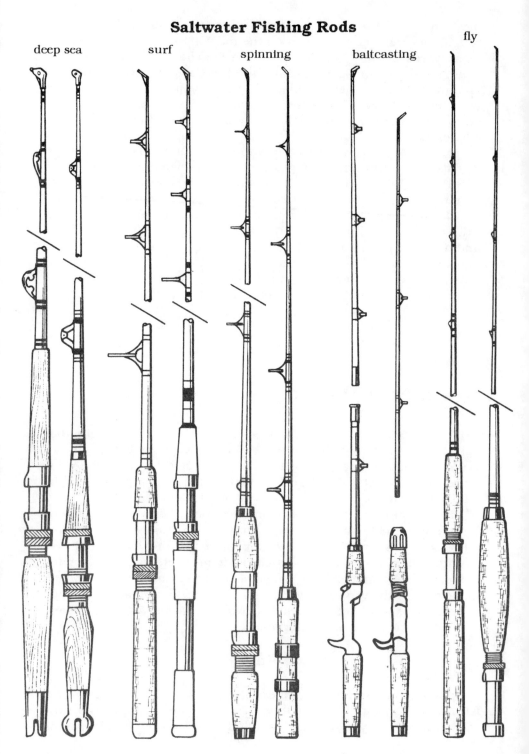

Saltwater Fishing Reels

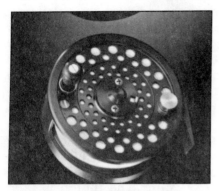

Orvis D-XR Fly Reel

Penn 440SS
Spinning Reel

Penn 25GLS Lever Drag
Casting Reel

Penn 9/0 Senator
Star Drag Reel

Penn International II
80 TW Trolling Reel

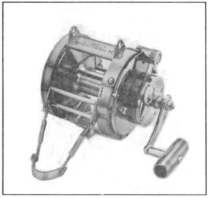

Penn International 130S
Two-Speed Big Game Reel

left hand if you are left handed). With the other hand reel the bait to about five inches from the end of the rod. Release the bail with the non-casting hand. With your index finger hold the line between the reel and the first guide. With an easy motion raise the rod tip to a position past the vertical slightly behind your head. Bring the rod forward, releasing the line, and cast the lure. Then continue to hold the rod in your primary hand and retrieve the lure by cranking the reel handle with your other hand. Most spinning reels are easily changed for operation with either hand by changing the handle from one side of the reel to the other. Soon you will be trying side arm casting and other techniques to fit a specific situation.

Most anglers cast a spinning rig with the line held close to the reel face with the index finger. Recently some skippers in the Florida Keys have been teaching that holding the line on top of the rod with the thumb is a more accurate method of casting. The thumb is then pointing in the direction of the cast and the line is released smoothly.

Spinning gear is used for casting from a bank, bridge, and a boat. When you try trolling with a spinning rod you will appreciate the versatility of this tool. A spinning rod and reel loaded with 250 to 350 yards of 12-pound test line is a thrilling trolling rig, and good sport for anything from a 4-pound bonito to a 40-pound sailfish.

The Rod. Unless portability is an overwhelming criterion, always buy a one-piece rod. A two-piece, or ferruled, rod lacks the smooth curve over the entire length that exists in a one-piece rod. Use different rods for different fishing methods. An ultra light rod (4- to 6-pound test line) is fun for snappers and grunts. A medium rod (8- to 12-pound) is good for barracuda, dolphin, bonefish, permit, small tunas and king-fish. Use a heavy rod for trolling for billfish, or use a 12-pound outfit. Heavy rods lack the flexibility needed for casting, so a 12-pound rod is a good first choice.

You will probably buy a rod and reel at the same time. This gives you the opportunity to try the outfit in the store. Mount the reel, put on a short length of line with a washer or other weight as the lure. Try a short cast to see how the rod reacts and how the rod and reel match. If the clerk gets upset, leave!

Some "whip" is desirable for smooth casting, but too much rod flexibility will interfere when you are fighting a fish. Close the bail and tie the end of the line to a fixed object. This will let you feel how the rod reacts with a "fish" on the line. The arc of the rod should be smooth and you should feel the pull from the object.

You can judge the quality of the rod by the same means discussed in the section on the baitcasting rod.

The Reel. As long as the parts of the reel that come into contact with the line are smooth, you can cast with almost any reel. The line will be moving over the surface of the reel and can be nicked or cut if the parts are not smooth.

However, the differences between reels become apparent after you have hooked a fish. With your line tied to a fixed object, raise the rod over your head and walk away from the object, but keep your eye on the rod tip. If the reel has a good drag system, the line will come off the reel smoothly without causing the rod tip to jerk. When you are fighting a fish you want the line to come off the reel smoothly so you can keep pressure on the fish without worrying about a jerky reel snapping the line.

The washers behind the spool that holds the line, control the drag of the spinning reel. On all other reels bait—casting, surfcasting, fly-casting and trolling—the drag washers are inside the frame of the reel. Some of the washers are made of metal to dissipate heat from friction; others will be leather, rubber like, asbestos, or most commonly today, teflon or a composite material. These washers must be kept clean and free of nicks. If they become nicked or scratched, gently polish them or replace them.

Next comes the question of lubrication. It is rare to find a salesperson or tackle shop proprietor who can give good advice on the subject. Follow the manufacturer's recommendation in the printed instructions that come with the reel. Some drag washers are not to be lubricated. Others may require light machine oil or light grease. Many modern reels have washers that are permanently lubricated with a dry graphite-type lubricant, and therefore should not be oiled or greased. Many manufacturers will specifically list the parts that require lubrication—if the maker does not tell you to oil the washers, don't! Regardless of the type of reel, you will have to maintain the drag system. Check the drag of your reel before every day of fishing.

Avoid closed-face spinning reels—they do not have the line capacity needed for saltwater action and are difficult to clean. All open-faced spinning reels are excellent beginners gear, but be certain that the reel is made for salt water. Freshwater reels corrode quickly in a saltwater environment.

The drag adjustment can be on the front (face) of the reel or on the rear. Either is fine, as long as the drag is set before you cast! Never change the drag while fighting a fish. Preset the drag at or about 1/3 of the pound test of the line you are using. If you have 12-pound test, set the drag at or about four pounds. Attach the line from your rod and reel to a light-weight bucket. Since a pint of water is about a pound, put four pints of water in the bucket and lift it with the rod. Set the drag so it will just lift the bucket. Now feel the pull of the drag with your hand. With practice, you can feel 3, 4, 5, or 6 pounds of pressure.

Baitcasting Gear

The technique of baitcasting is much simpler than spincasting, but achieving a good cast is more difficult. Hold the rod in your primary

11

hand and with the lure at the tip of the rod and the reel handles pointing straight up. Bring the rod past the overhead vertical and cast forward while snapping the wrist. Now comes the problem, backlash! When the lure hits the water the spool of the reel is still turning rapidly. The result is that without proper intervention on your part, the line will continue coming off the reel. This causes the line to tangle on the reel. With experience you will learn to first, slow the spool, and then when the lure hits the water stop the spinning spool with your thumb.

Modern baitcasting reels have a system of magnetic brakes to prevent backlash. Most of these work somewhat, but your proficiency at casting is still needed to avoid backlash. After a successful cast you retrieve the line, changing the rod from the primary hand to your other hand and cranking the reel handle with your primary hand.

While spinning reels are easy to change from right to left hand operation, baitcasting reels are not easy to alter. If you want a left-handed reel, you will have to buy one.

The Reel. The baitcasting reel also should have a drag system that is smooth. A simple test of the drag is to tie on a few yards of line, then hold the line to suspend the reel in the air. You can adjust the drag so the reel will smoothly slide to the floor. A modern good quality reel will have a free spool feature that allows the spool to turn while the handles remain stationery. Or you can select a reel with a level wind feature as an option. The level wind does not seem to reduce casting distance and therefore is a desirable reel feature. All modern reels have an adjustable drag mechanism so you can match the drag to the weight of the lure.

The Rod. Until recently baitcasting rigs that could cast small lures were not available. Now new ultra-light rigs are available that will cast a lure as small as a 1/8 of an ounce jig used for bonefishing. Baitcasting rods are shorter and stiffer than spinning rods. As with spinning gear, the feel of the rod and reel together is of prime concern. Mount the chosen reel on the rod and check the balance and feel. With either a spinning or baitcasting rig the point of balance of a well matched rod and reel should be 4 to 6 inches above the reel seat towards the tip of the rod. Supported at this point the rod and reel should balance from the butt to tip without falling.

Check the quality of the rod by first looking down the rod from the butt through the rod guides. The rod guides should line up perfectly. The reel seat should be made of strong non-corrosive material. Chrome on brass is good, but anodized aluminum and space-age plastics are also strong. The reel seat should have double locking screws.

The guides should be double wrapped. The first wrap is under the guides, the second is over the feet of the guides. The finish of the rod is more than just an aesthetic consideration. The finish will largely determine the life of the rod. The cheapest finish is a varnish into which the entire rod, including guides, is dipped. Better rods will have the finish applied before the guides are attached. Either type of finish should be glossy and free of flaws. Decorative wraps and color are a matter of personal choice. Select a single-piece rod over a two-piece rod, although this consideration is not as important as it is with a spinning rod. Many baitcasting rods disassemble at the butt so the rod joint does not interfere with the smooth curve of the rod. The handle, or grip, of a saltwater fishing rod is not offset, but aligns in a straight line with the rod.

Flyfishing Gear

Saltwater fly fishing is rapidly gaining popularity. Until recent years, only a few specialists used this very light-weight tackle for the larger saltwater fish species. Now more than 25% of the sales of fly fishing gear is for saltwater use. The drag systems now used in fly fishing reels have advanced enough to fight large fish, but the fly rod is still the most important part of the system. For fly fishing the balance between the two components is more important than in the other types of fishing.

The Rod. A fly fishing rod with the line is almost like a long whip. The flow of motion from the tip of the rod should be passed on to the line. Therefore, the rod must have a soft and whip-like action, but without any rod vibrations after the casting action. Smoothly cast the rod forward; the tip should continue easily with the line of the cast and return to a straight position with a bare minimum of vibration.

The guides on the fly rod increase friction on the line, slowing the movement of the line. Therefore, the fewer guides the better. The guides must be in a straight line, and be as light weight as possible.

Fly rods are called fast or slow, but this does not refer to the flexibility of the rod. It refers to whether the flexibility starts in the butt area, slow action, or is concentrated in the tip section, fast action. It is easier to learn with a slow action rod.

When an angler speaks of a fly rod as light, medium or heavy, he is talking about the weight of the line used in a balanced outfit. Most salt water rigs are either medium or heavy, between 8 and 9-1/2 feet long. The shorter medium gear is used for bonefish, permit, and sea trout; the longer and heavier gear is for tarpon and sailfish.

The Reel. The reel must be built for salt water. Other important factors are that the reel must have an adjustable drag system, and a large enough line capacity for the long runs of the saltwater species you will be after. The first run of a hooked bonefish can be more than 400 feet; if the line capacity of your reel is 100 feet you will come up short. Test the drag system as you would for spinning or baitcasting rigs.

Surfcasting Gear

The proper gear for surf casting is a long heavy rod, and a heavy, high capacity reel either of the bait casting type, or, more commonly, open-faced spinning reels. However, never miss the chance to fish an active surf because you don't have a surf rod and reel. Surf casting even with ultra-light spinning tackle can be a thrill. Sometimes you will be casting 6 to 8 ounces of whole squid, with a weight attached; other times you will cast jigs as light as 2 ounces. After a little experience, you will want two sets of surf casting gear.

The Rod. The surf rod will be a heavy, stout rod with a very long butt. The butt is built for two-handed casting and should be about 24 inches long. The guides add friction when casting, so the first guide in surf spinning tackle should be about 35 inches above the butt, whereas in conventional tackle about 25 inches above the butt is sufficient. In either case there should be 4 to 6 guides. The overall length of a surf rod can range from 8 to 15 feet. Most rods will be about 10 feet long.

The Reel. A conventional surf casting reel will have a "star" drag system so the drag can be adjusted to the conditions of the surf and the fish you are after. The reel, either spinning or conventional, will have a capacity of several hundred yards of 30-pound test line. The open faced spinning reel must have an adjustable drag system — they all do — and the line must flow off the reel easily, since you will be attempting very long casts.

Trolling Gear

Any good 12-pound test or heavier baitcasting or spinning rig will make a good trolling rig. However there are many rod and reel combinations that are designed specifically for trolling.

The Rod. There are two distinct types of rods made for trolling, both are called boat rods. A traditional type of boat rod is moderately stiff and six or seven feet long. The stiffness makes it unsuitable for casting. The butt has two grooves for seating in rod holders or in a fighting chair. The other type of boat rod is intended to be held while standing and fighting a fish. This rod is shorter, about 5 feet long, and even stiffer. Fighting a fish while standing is very effective for fish up to a 70-pound sailfish or white marlin. If you are after bigger quary, the traditional fighting chair with a harness may be necessary. For either type of fishing a rod belt with a butt holder can help.

The Reel. Most trolling reels are 20-pound test or heavier, and most use a star drag. The star drag type of trolling reels have a lever to select either a preset drag, set by the star, or free spool. You will select free spool while trolling and engage the drag when you want to set the hook in a fish. Once the drag has been preset it should not be changed while fighting a fish. When the reel is in free spool you must have the line held by a clothespin or some other type of outrigger clip. More sophisticated reels have a lever which permits you to set a drag for trolling and another preset drag for fighting the fish. The choice here is usually a matter of cost. The star drag reels are normally sized 4/0, 6/0, 9/0 and so on, and prices start at about $80. The 4/0 is suitable for 20-pound test line, the 9/0 is used with up to 50-pound test line. The reels with multiple adjustable drags are sized as 20, 30, 50 and up, and the prices start at about $250. The size of the reel corresponds to the pound test of the line to be used with the reel.

Knots

There are a few standard terms which are used when describing knots. The standing part of the line is the long length of the line; in fishing knots it is usually the line from the reel. The bitter end is the short piece of line on the end that is used to tie the knot. When tying a knot, its maximum strength will be achieved if you keep the pieces of line parallel and keep spirals neat. Use special knots for tying a fifty-pound test leader to a ten-pound test line. Tying twenty- or thirty-pound test leader on a ten-pound test line should not present any problems if you moisten the knot with your tongue and pull the knot steadily to tighten it. Sketches of many of the conventional fishing knots follow. You will need some particular knots in specific situations. An example: use the Stu Apte Improved Blood Knot when tying a very heavy leader to the lighter line on your reel. However there are few simple knots that will serve most of your needs.

Basic Knots

Simple Loop Knot. This knot forms a standing loop in a leader that can be clipped to your line with a snap swivel.

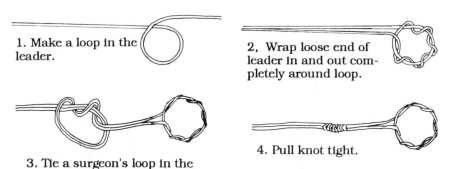

1. Make a loop in the leader.

2. Wrap loose end of leader in and out completely around loop.

3. Tie a surgeon's loop in the double line below the loop.

4. Pull knot tight.

The Surgeon's End Loop. This easy knot will form a double line of any length. If the loop is longer than three feet, add another regular surgeon's knot within 36 inches of the end of the loop. The loop serves two purposes. The first is to form a loop for attaching your lure, hook or snap swivel. Second, it provides added strength since if the double line is longer than the length of the rod, the double line is on the reel before the leader hits the tip of the rod.

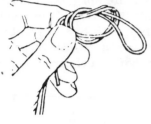

1. Double end of line to form loop and tie overhand knot at base of double line.

2. Leave loop open in knot and bring doubled line through once more.

3. Hold standing line and tag end and pull loop to tighten knot. Size of loop can be determined by pulling loose knot to desired point and holding it while knot is tightened.

The Palomar Knot. This knot attaches a hook or lure to your looped line.

1. Double about 4 inches of line and pass loop through eye.

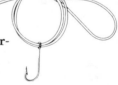

2. Let hook hang loose and tie overhand knot in doubled line. Avoid **twisting** lines and don't tighten.

3. Pull loop of line far enough to pass it over hook, swivel or lure. Make sure loop passes completely over this attachment.

4. Pull both tag end and standing line to tighten. Clip tag end.

Offshore Swivel Knot. This knot attaches a swivel, snap swivel, hook, lure or leader to the looped line.

1. Slip loop end of double-line leader through eye of swivel. Rotate loop end a half-turn to put a single twist between loop and swivel eye.

2. Pass the loop with the twist over the swivel. Hold end of the loop, plus both legs of the double-line leader with one hand. Let swivel slide to other end of double loops now formed.

3. Still holding loop and lines with one hand, use other to rotate swivel through center of both loops, at least six times.

4. Continue holding both legs of double-line leader tightly but release end of loop. Pull on swivel and loops will begin to gather.

5. To draw knot tight, grip swivel with pliers and push loops toward eye with fingers, while still keeping standing lines of the leader pulled tight.

The Surgeon's Knot. This version ties a heavy leader to your fishing line.

1. Lay line and leader parallel, overlapping 6-8".

2. Treating the two like a single line, tie an overhand knot, pulling the entire leader through the loop.

3. Leaving the loop of the overhand open, pull both tag end of line and leader through again.

4. Hold both lines and both ends to pull knot tight. Clip ends close to avoid foul-up in rod guides.

Other Knots

Stu Apte Improved Blood Knot. Ties a heavy to a much lighter fishing line.

1. Double a sufficient length of the smaller diameter line so that it can be wrapped around the standing part of the larger diameter line with 6 turns out and 5 turns back in toward the beginning of the wrap. The 5 turns back are made over the top of the initial 6 turns.

2. Hold the looped line between the thumb and the forefinger at "X", to keep from unwinding.

3. Wind the larger diameter line around the standing part of the double line 3 times, but in opposite direction. Insert the end upwards through the loop at the same point "X". Note: Wrap a napkin or any protective piece of material around forefingers before pulling up the knot, since it is difficult to pull this knot up firmly. Wet the knot with saliva.

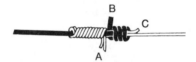

4. Pull the knot up slowly and tightly to keep it from slipping. Both sides of this "jam" knot should come together at the same time.

5. Cut off the ends of the double loop (A) and the end of the heavy line (B), both about 1/8" from the knot. Cut off the loose end of the double line (C) about 1/8" from the knot.

Hook Snell. Allows several hooks to be attached to your line.

1. Thread line through hook eye about 6 inches. Hold line against hook shank and form circle.

2. Make as many turns through loop and around line and shank as desired. Close knot by pulling on tag end of line.

3. Tighten by pulling standing line in one direction and hook in the other.

Bimini Twist. This is the strongest knot used to form a double line.

1. Measure a little more than twice the footage you'll want for the double-line leader. Bring end back to standing line and hold together. Rotate end of loop 20 times, putting twists in it.

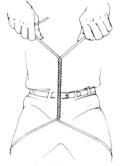

2. Spread loop to force twists together about 10 inches below tag end. Step both feet through loop and bring it up around knees so pressure can be placed on column of twists by spreading knees apart.

3. With twists forced tightly together, hold standing line in one hand with tension just slightly off the vertical. With other hand, move tag end to position at right angle to twists. Keeping tension on loop with knees, gradually ease tension of tag end so it will roll over the column of twists, beginning just below the upper twist.

4. Spread legs apart slowly to maintain pressure on loop. Steer tag end into a tight coil as it continues to roll over the twisted line.

5. When spiral of tag end has rolled over column of twists, continue keeping knee pressure on loop and move hand which has held standing line down to grasp knot. Place finger in crotch of line where loop joins knot to prevent slippage of last turn. Take half hitch with tag end around nearest leg of loop and pull up tight.

6. With half-hitch holding knot, release knee pressure but keep loop stretched out tight. Using remaining tag end, take half-hitch around both legs of loop, but do not pull tight.

7. Make two more turns with the tag end around both legs of the loop, winding inside the bend of line formed by the loose half-hitch and toward the main knot. Pull tag end slowly, forcing the 3 loops to gather in a spiral.

8. When loops are pulled up neatly against main knot, tighten to lock knot in place. Trim tag end about 1/4" from knot.

These directions apply to tying double-line leaders of around 5 feet or less. For longer double-line sections, two people may be required to hold the line and make initial twists.

Improved Clinch Knot. Ties a hook to your line.

1. Pass line through eye of hook, swivel, or lure.
Double back and make 5 turns around the
standing line. Hold coils in place; thread end of
line around first loop above eye, then through big
loop as shown.

2. Hold tag end and standing line while coils are pulled up.
Take care that coils are in spiral, not lapping over each
other. Slide tight against eye. Clip tag end.

Terminal Tackle

The first decision is whether to use a wire leader or a monofilament leader. Monofilament will get more hits, but you will lose some kingfish, barracuda and sharks. The more hardware on your terminal tackle, the fewer hits you will get. This is less true of offshore trolling than any other type of fishing. The use of swivels and snaps for trolling gear can be argued at length. The use of swivels reduces the problem of twisted lines when trolling. Leaders and baits can be changed more easily and quickly if snap swivels are used. There is good evidence that such conveniences do reduce the catch when trolling. Nothing is as easy as having your fishing line end with a snap swivel, and all your baits and lures rigged with a swivel at the beginning of the leader, but this convenience has its price. For most varieties of fish tie your bait directly to your double line with a palomar or offshore knot.

You will need a leader when fishing for billfish. Select 80-pound test monofilament as your leader for sailfish, or 200-pound test for larger billfish. Tie the monofilament leader to the doubled fishing line—use a double surgeon's knot to tie a long loop in your leader and use the offshore knot or the palomar knot to tie your lure to the leader. Do this before you leave the dock. It is of prime importance to be ready to fish when you see the weeds, or the birds, or the free jumping sailfish.

The lure should always be tied directly to the shock leader of a flyline. On light spinining or light baitcasting rigs, always tie the line to the lure, jig, crank bait, hook or plug. Fish will avoid the extra hardware of swivels and snaps and you will catch fewer fish if you use them.

In surf casting several types of swivels and weights are used. When using heavier spinning, baitcasting, or trolling gear, the decision is not so clear. When using these rigs to bottom fish, the use of swivels and snaps is very convenient, and doesn't reduce the catch.

Whether you are fishing the bottom, bridges or cuts, or drifting—all are productive, but you must be ready! If you must stop to rig, your opportunity will pass before you are ready. Most of the rigging for a successful fishing trip is done onshore, before the trip.

The Lures

Live Baitfish

Any small live fish is an excellent bait, if treated properly. Even saltwater catfish can be a good bait if the spines are cut off of the fish's back. The live bait you use will depend on what is available. You can buy live fish, net live baitfish and most often catch them with a small hook and small pieces of either squid or shelled shrimp. If you have acquired the skills, it is fun to net baitfish when you find them. What is the best baitfish? The one you can get easily!

After you have caught any live bait — crabs, shrimp, or small fish — it is important to keep the bait live and lively. A constant supply of aerated water is essential. Shrimp or crabs can be easily maintained in a simple bait bucket which is kept in salt water. Live baitfish are more difficult to keep, and require an aerator running continually in a live well. Adding fresh salt water to the live well periodically also helps. But temperature is also important: water that is either too cool or too hot will make the bait less lively. Keep the baitfish fresh and fast moving and you will catch more fish.

Blue runners and goggle eyes are good baitfish, and durable. Mullet are at least as good, but care must be taken since they are fragile and easily injure themselves inside a closed container. Pilchards, pinfish and grunts work well.

There are as many ways to rig live baitfish as there are species available. These fish are usually used while trolling or drifting. In either case it is better to have some baits swimming on the surface and some swimming deep. If you want a bait to stay on top of the water, rig it through the lips or the very top of the eye socket. Hook the baits you want to swim down at or behind the dorsal fin. Adding a sinker of one or two ounces will help keep the baitfish down.

There are two aids which help keep the fish at or near the surface. The easiest is a simple child's balloon inflated and tied to the leader or swivel. This makes it simple to follow the path of each baitfish. A kite rig is very effective for catching most offshore fishes (see page 60). Fly a good steady kite down wind from the boat from any spare rod and reel filled with 20- or 30-pound test line. The line from the rod with the baitfish is run through a clothespin or snap hanging from the kite line. This allows you to reduce or increase the amount of line in order to keep the baitfish splashing at the surface of the water.

Shrimp

Netting shrimp at night can be a rewarding sport, but you will probably eat most, if not all, of the shrimp you catch. Therefore shrimp used for bait are usually bought at a bait shop. Live shrimp are an excellent bait for many coastal saltwater species. It is always desirable to keep the shrimp lively, but some species of fish are not as fussy as others. If you are fishing for snook, tarpon, or sometimes even redfish, it is necessary that the shrimp be lively. Hook the shrimp just under the bony ridge on the head when fishing for these species. Avoid the black spot visible on the side of the shrimp. When hooked this way, the shrimp will stay lively for a reasonable length of time, as long as it was lively when first hooked.

However, such sprightly shrimp are not always necessary for snapper or bottom feeding fish. For these fish carefully thread the shrimp on the hook. This will restrict the movement of the bait severely. So much so that you can use dead bait just as effectively, so that any left over live shrimp from a fishing trip can be saved for another day by careful freezing. This saves money and frozen shrimp can be used effectively on popping corks for sea trout as well as fishing the bottom for snapper or grouper. A threaded shrimp is much harder for small fish to steal than is a shrimp hooked through the head.

A few live shrimp in a chum bar (see page 35) can attract fish with the noise they make.

Crabs and Sand Fleas

When fishing for tarpon, permit, snapper or grouper two special baits are quite effective. Small blue crabs about 1 to 1-1/2 inches across make excellent bait for tarpon or permit; larger blue crabs can be very effective for bottom fishing for grouper or snapper. Sand fleas are any of the small crustaceans found at the shore that jump about like fleas when disturbed or caught. These are the most effective bait for pompano or sometimes even permit, snook or tarpon. Both of these baits can be fished from a boat, pier or surf.

Rigged Bait

Pieces of shrimp, squid or any cut up fish make good baits when fishing for grouper, snapper, baitfish, or any bottom fish. Simply cut these into bite-sized hunks, hook them securely and fish. Squid is plentiful, cheap and easily obtained at any bait store. It is very tough so it is also the hardest for the small bait stealers to pick off your hook. However, in the normal course of fishing you will end up with plenty of the other baits which can be frozen and used at another time. Have the bait cut to size before you freeze the pieces in a plastic bag or wrap them in plastic.

Buy rigged baitfish such as balao (ballyhoo), mullet, and blue runners from the bait shops. Or you can rig and freeze left over live baits into excellent trolling or drifting baits. Whether you rig the baits or purchase them, you will have to make two decisions.

The first decision is whether to use a wire or monofilament leader. If your quarry is either kingfish or barracuda, you must use wire or lose most of the fish you hook. For most other fishes, including billfish, monofilament is preferred—you will get more hook-ups and not lose too many fish. The next consideration is the number of hooks in the rigged bait. If you want more hook-ups, stick to a single hook rigged bait except for kingfish; for kingfish use three hooks. If you choose a rig with two hooks, decide whether to rig with the second hook in the same direction, at a 90 degree angle, or at 180 degrees to the first hook. Two hooks in the same direction or at 180 degrees add some stability to the running of the lure.

To rig most baitfish tie a hook, 4/0 to 8/0 depending on the fish you are after, to about 6 feet of 50- to 80-pound test monofilament with a palomar knot. Use the same knot to tie a swivel on the other end of the line. Pass the hook through the mouth of the bait and push the hook out the gill. Wire the mouth shut and wire the fish to the eye of the hook, and the bait is ready for use. It is a good idea to form loose 5-inch coils of the leader, place the bait in plastic and freeze it. Now the bait is ready whenever you can fish. Thaw the bait in a bucket of salt water before using it, and be sure that the thawed bait will have good action by flexing the fish several times before attaching the leader to your fishing line.

Another excellent method of rigging baitfish is to pass a 6-inch length of Monel wire through the very top of the baitfish's eye socket and twist the line securely tight. Then pass the ends of the wire around the hook and again twist tightly. With a little practice this is a fast and tight method of rigging.

typical two-hook rigged ballyhoo

Often the local bait shop will only have baits rigged with two hooks and wire leader. These will work too, but the two-hook rig will reduce the swimming action of your bait. The wire will sometimes reduce the number of hook-ups. Most bait shops will make baits up for your special instructions, but you must order ahead. It is frequently easier to rig them yourself.

Special Rigs

A favorite kingfish rig is a 2- or 3-ounce yellow jig with three hooks. Put the eye of the second hook over the point of the jig hook and close the hook eye; do the same again, hooking the eye of the third hook over the point of the second. Then tip the rig with a piece of dead bait, a whole small fish, a strip of baitfish, a strip of squid, or even a large shrimp. Troll this slowly over the local kingfish hole and await results. Anchoring with a chum line makes the rig even more effective.

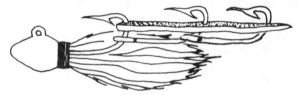

special three-hook jig for kingfish

Similarly a jig or spoon, single hook, with strip of bait or even a plastic strip, available at tackle shops, is effective trolled, cast or deep jigged.

There are a myriad plugs, spoons, and jigs designed to be cast, trolled or jigged. Many are good baits in specific situations. Most artificial lures rely on colors to attract the fish. If you are using these, have many colors available and keep changing until you find the color that is working that day.

Colored skirts have a definite use with dead trolled baits. They use color to attract, and your dead baits will be life like longer if you use skirts. Skirts also help keep your rigged bait from picking up weed. Again have many colors ready, and change them until you find the one that the fish like.

If your game is billfish, consider high speed trolling with large artificial lures. Very successful billfishermen use this technique with good results! High speed is from 12 to 20 knots. At this speed it is futile to try dead baits, since they will just break apart at high speed. For this sport you will use durable hard and soft plastic lures. These are in the form of "birds" that skim and fly from the wake, all kinds of artificial fish, multiple chains of plastic squid, plastic plugs and lures of all shapes and sizes.

Whatever lures you use be certain that the lures and lines match your game. Use 200-pound test mono leader and number 10/0 hooks for marlin; 80 pound test mono leader and a 5/0 hook for sailfish and dolphin; 50 pound test mono leader, 1/0 or 2/0 hooks for grouper, snook, snapper, and redfish; 1/0 hooks and wire leaders for bluefish; and about a #2 hook and 20-pound test leader for sea trout.

Where To Fish

You can fish almost any where there is salt or brackish water. Fishing is productive from bridges or banks of rivers or canals, on bays and flats, from bridges over bays and inlets, and from almost any kind of boat. You can cast, still fish, bottom fish, drift or troll.

Drift Boats or Head Boats

In any saltwater fishing area there will be boats of this type. In some areas they are called head boats, in other areas they are called drift boats or party boats. These boats offer fine offshore fishing at a very reasonable price. Most of these boats supply rods and reels and bait suitable for the fish they are after, or you can bring your own rig and bait. The boat will be out for about 4 or 8 hours, so you want to bring something cold to drink, and maybe even a sandwich. There will be one or two mates on board to help you.

The mates will help you rig, supply baits if needed, and give you whatever aid you require. They will mark the fish you catch, and at the end of the trip they will clean them for you. As in all service businesses, you should tip the helper or mate for the amount of help you received. The experienced drift fisherman will require no help, the novice may require a lot of help. If you are a novice and need help, a $10 tip should be in line, plus a couple of bucks for each fish that is cleaned.

Most of the time you will be bottom fishing with cut bait. However some drift boats even permit kite fishing with live bait. Ask about the type of fishing before you leave the dock.

On any of these boats some excellent catches are made. If someone is fighting a sailfish or other large catch, you may be asked to bring in your lines to allow the fisherman a better chance to fight the fish. Bring your lines in quickly if asked. The kind of fish you will catch depends on whether you are fishing day or night and the season of the year, but you can expect to catch grouper, snapper, kingfish, bluefish, and maybe even billfish. Release any fish that won't be eaten. On most drift boats someone will take a fish that you don't want. On drift boats as on charter fishing boats, someone may try to talk you into mounting your catch, and in the excitement of the moment you will be tempted. Stop and consider, you will be killing a wonderful fish, and paying several hundred dollars for something you may not want.

Charter Boats

Aside from having your own fishing boat, this is the most expensive way to fish. The charter boats range from 26 feet to 60 feet, all come with a professional captain, and most have a mate or two. The captain is the boss, the mate or mates are there to help you and do the work—bait and let out lines, gaff fish, clean fish, *etc*. Charters are for either half or full days, and normally carry two to six anglers.

However remember you are hiring a professional captain and at least one mate for a full day, paying for the use of a $100,000 boat, and probably using 150 gallons of either diesel fuel or gasoline. So don't be shocked if you must pay between $600 and $1,000 for a full day's charter for four to six anglers. For that kind of money don't be shy. See the boat, meet the skipper, and see the rods and reels you will be using.

Charter boats are available for hire for fishing trips of one-half day, a full day or trips of several days or a week.

Both the skipper and the mate can teach you excellent techniques. Observe them carefully, and ask questions. If you decide to go for billfish, watch them work together to fly a kite. Notice where to place the teaser, the outrigger lines and the flat lines; check the trolling speed. If you go out on a half day charter with three other fishermen you can get more than $100 worth of lessons, and the pleasure will be free.

Wading

Fishing the shallow waters, commonly called the flats, of any bay, bayou, canal or river is inexpensive. Flats fishing requires great skill. The angler first must stalk the fish, and then offer it a lure without scaring the fish away. Most of the species caught this way are indisputably the prey of experts. In the shallow areas of bays you can catch sea trout. On the flats between the bays and the ocean there will be tarpon, permit, and bonefish. All are outstanding catches. Also available on the flats are the bonus fishes—sharks and barracuda. When fishing the flats most anglers use light or ultra-light tackle. Catching a small shark or barracuda on such a rig is excellent sport.

MONROE COUNTY TOURIST DEVELOPMENT COUNCIL

The prize of flats fishing, this bonefish was caught in the Florida Keys. Wading is one way of sneaking up on these extremely wary fish.

Fish in water six inches to waist deep. Usually, you will carry all the gear you need on your person. Be certain that you are wearing stout sport walking shoes to avoid cuts and stings. Watch where you walk. What looks like a dark weed patch could be a six-foot-deep hole. In all types of fishing sunburn can be a severe problem — wear long pants, a hat and a long-sleeved shirt. It is best to carry a staff of some sort so you can probe ahead when necessary. Normally all fish caught in this type of fishing are released, since there is no way to ice the fish, although some fishermen will go to some lengths to keep a few sea trout. The turn of the tide is most productive fishing time on any flat.

Bridges and Banks

This is a productive and social sport. On bridges over salt water everywhere, there are fishermen who will gladly share their secrets with any newcomer. One of the fine pleasures of bridge fishing is the easy companionship of the anglers. A 20-pound test rod and reel is most commonly used since your quarry can wrap your line around pilings, bridges and rocks. You will also need some cut bait, hooks and sinkers. Also a bucket or cooler is needed to keep your catch, your bait, and something cold to drink. Fish on the side of the bridge where

PLANO MOLDING CO.

Surf casting is a fishing method that does not require a boat, but still produces a variety of fishes including bluefish, striped bass, snook, and tarpon.

the tide carries your bait away from the bridge. Grunts, pinfish, snapper and occasionally tarpon can be found. At night you may find grouper and, in season, snook!

This same helpful friendly attitude is prevalent among the people fishing along banks. You will use the same equipment for banks as for bridges. The catch will vary depending on the salt content of the water, but besides panfish you can catch tarpon and snook even in brackish water.

Surf Casting

This is another inexpensive method of fishing, and the basic techniques are the same on the Atlantic, Pacific and Gulf coasts. Sometimes the action is furious, other times you can sit, smoke a pipe and swap tales with the others on the beach, and still be fishing. A strong two-handed cast is the standard method. The bait can be live bait, cut bait, or artificial lures. Fish in daylight or at night, whenever you can. In any light, cast directly into the white water churned by feeding bluefish or striped bass. Letting your sinker-weighted bait swim or drift can bring tarpon, snook, or barracuda out of an uneventful surf. When one of the schooling species is running, there will be plenty of other fishermen for companions; other times this can be a contemplative sport.

Small Boat Fishing, Inshore

A small boat increases the fisherman's range in any type of fishing. The small boat can get to the otherwise inaccessible flats for wading and can hold fish-keeping coolers and fishing gear nearby. It will get the angler to otherwise remote waters of canals and rivers. When you want to fish bay waters a small boat is practical. When fishing under mangroves, holes in the bay bottom, or oyster beds the small boat will get you there. In any small boat 18 feet or less you can run through sheltered waters to find the foremost fishing grounds.

Depending on the prudence and skill of the boater, a boat of 12 to 18 feet is suitable—you can cast for drum, troll for sea trout, fly fish for tarpon, or wade for permit. The typical bass boat can be rigged for double duty and provide an excellent fishing platform for salt water. At one time or another you will probably end up in some remote spot and lose track of the time. And more than likely you will end up high and dry because the tide has run out. Because these are all tidal waters, you must be aware of the tides at all times. Never venture into new waters without a current navigational chart and a compass.

The fine-eating redfish is one of the many species of saltwater fishes that can be caught while backcountry fishing in a small boat.

One of the big thrills of offshore fishing is fighting a blue marlin. High speed trolling with large artificial lures is one method of finding these exciting gamefish.

Offshore Fishing

Many boats larger than 18 feet are designed for offshore fishing. By exercising some judgement, any of the boats designed for offshore work can be used safely. Prudence is required. Never venture offshore without the required safety equipment and a working marine radio on which you can call for help when needed. With good judgment you will never have to use the radio except to hear where and when the fish are hitting. Never assume that just because a boat is 26 feet long it is suitable for offshore fishing, since it may be in poor running condition and lack necessary safety gear. Offshore fishing is anywhere on the open ocean, even 400 yards from shore in 15 feet of water.

Offshore game will be grouper and snapper when bottom fishing; or cast for bluefish in 20 to 100 feet of water, troll or fish live or cut bait in 60 to 90 feet for kingfish, cobia, wahoo or tripletail. At or near inlets tarpon and barracuda are caught using live bait, trolling lures or casting lures. You will find amberjack, grouper and big snapper over wrecks and artificial reefs in 60 to 100 feet. The search for sailfish starts in 100 to 120 feet of water fishing with either live bait, or trolling

SANDRA ROMASHKO

Allison tuna, also called yellowfin tuna, (left) and barracuda are two more offshore species. The tuna puts up an arm-breaking fight and often merely strips all the line off the reel.

rigged baits and lures, but look for the color change where the water turns from green to blue. You will also regularly find sharks when fishing for sailfish.

In the Atlantic, the big offshore fish species are found in the Gulf Stream. The Gulf Stream meanders so its location varies from day to day and season to season. In winter months the weather stations of the National Oceanographic and Atmospheric Administration broadcast the approximate position of the Gulf Stream. However, even with this information you will still have to visually search for this current of water in the middle of the ocean. In the Gulf Stream the water is usually rougher or quieter than the surrounding seas, the color is a slightly darker blue, and most of the year the water is warmer. The fish in the Gulf Stream are tunas, blue marlin, and dolphin, and trolling is the way to locate them.

Techniques and Conditions That Affect Fishing

Sun, Moon and Tides

Fishing in all salt or brackish water is strongly affected by these three factors. Never begin a fishing trip without knowing the status of the sun or moon and the tides. The position of the sun, the moon and the earth determine the levels of the tides. The illumination of the sun and the moon also appears to affect fishing. The tides have a definite effect on fishes' feeding habits. Some prefer the incoming, rising or flood tide, while other species prefer the outgoing, falling or ebb tide. The high-water slack period, when there is little or no flow, occurs at the highest point of the tide. At the lowest point, the low-water slack period occurs. The time for each cycle from high to low tide is about 6 hours and 12-1/2 minutes, so there are 4 such cycles each tidal day which is about 24 hours and 50 minutes.

Also during each lunar month there is an unusually large range between the high and low tides called the spring tide. Each lunar month there is similarly a small range between high and low tide called a neap tide. Fishing activity increases with the high rate of water flow of the spring tides.

Sailfish and dolphin are typical of fish that can be found by looking for specific fishing conditions. The sailfish was caught in 120 feet of water on a blustery day with the wind blowing from the north; the dolphin was found in a school under a weed patch which accumulated in a current.

The changing light at sunrise and sunset also acts to increase the activity of fish. Some fish feed at night, some feed primarily during the day. Both night feeders and day feeders become active at the times of the changing light. And changing tides also enhance the feeding activity of the fish. The net effect of this is that a changing tide at dawn or dusk can be the most productive time to fish.

Similarly the light of the moon appears to stimulate the feeding of the night feeders—the brighter the moon, the more activity. So the changing of the tide when the moon is brightest is a good time to fish.

Artificial light also attracts and stimulates fishes' feeding activity. Fish can be found wherever lights hit the water, so fishing under bridges at night can be very productive. Normally fishing is very good on the down-tide side of the lighted bridge.

However none of this is cast in steel. Use this information as a beginning point, but build your own records. Use a calendar to check the phase of the moon and the newspaper to check tides, sunrise, sunset, moonrise and moonset. Now start your own record of what you caught, when, and where. Also record the status of the sun, the moon, and the tides. With accumulation of these records you can predict when a fishing trip will be successful.

Currents

Currents play a major role in fishing. The big current in the eastern United States is the Gulf Stream. It enters the Gulf of Mexico at the Yucatan Peninsula, forms a large loop in the eastern Gulf, and exits at the Straits of Florida. The Gulf Stream then flows north almost to Cape Hatteras, where it turns northeast to just south of the Grand Banks of Newfoundland. This immense current affects fishing from east of the West Indies near the Sargasso Sea to the North Atlantic.

Lesser currents also affect fishing. Fast rising rip currents will drag baitfish in the upward flow. If you can spot these flows, you will find feeding fish among weeds and detritus accumulated in these currents.

Weed Lines

Dip your net into a clump of sargassum weeds, and you will understand why fishing under weed lines is so good. Your net will have several species of small marine life. The baitfish congregate here and the gamefish gather to feed on the baitfish. One of the prime places to find a marlin is under a feeding school of dolphin. Understanding the food chain will help you locate good fishing grounds.

Birds

You can spot birds at sea from a considerable distance and their activity will indicate whether or not feeding fish are present. Ignore birds that are out looking for fish. These birds will fly a circuitous course, occasionally dipping close to the water for a closer look. Birds that are actually feeding will act nervous, then dive into the water. Feeding birds will emit a high pitched squeal. Always fish around feeding birds.

Chum

Chumming is a technique used to stimulate the appetite of the fish before they hit your bait. There are several types of chum.

The most used chum is either chopped fish parts frozen in a large block, or freshly ground on the boat when you start fishing. In either case the chum will end up in a bucket with salt water. Slowly dip half-cup portions into the water. The boat should be up current from the fishing area so the stream of chopped fish and fish oil will drift down current from the boat towards your bait. Chumming offshore over a reef is very effective for kingfish and other mackerel.

Or you can use a chum bag, in which you place the solid, undiluted chum in a mesh bag. Tie the bag to the boat and place it overboard so that the odor of the chum drifts toward the baits. This method is somewhat easier than dispensing the chum in the water, and does not feed the fish on the way to your baits. The chum bag is most effective over a wreck or reef, where you are trying to coax the fish out of their hiding places.

A chum bar is a third method. First you must make a chum bar. Take an 8 inch long, 1-2 inch diameter PVC pipe nipple threaded on both ends. Drill 1/4 inch holes on the shank of the pipe; cap both ends, after drilling a 1/8 inch hole in one cap. Pass a line through the drilled cap to attach the bar to the boat. Fill the bar with any chum, including live shrimp. If you use ground or frozen chum, the bar will allow some small amounts of chum and the odor to drift down current. If you use a few live shrimp, the sound of the shrimp and the odor will attract the fish to the boat. Sometimes gamefish can be seen coming right up to the chum bar. The chum bar can be cast toward a patch reef and slowly reeled back to the boat leaving a scent the fish can follow.

Liquid chum is sold in all tackle shops. Lures are dipped into this chum to make the lure more desireable to fish. Sometimes liquid chum can be dipped into the water like regular chum, but you will want to do this prudently since the liquid chum is rather expensive.

You can make chum balls by mixing ground fish and sand. The balls can be frozen or made in the boat. When bottom fishing a fresh chum ball made up of ground fish and sand and packed like a snowball, is dropped over the side and slowly disintegrates as it sinks. This can be very effective for yellowtails, grouper and snapper. For schooling offshore fishes—tuna, dolphin, and kingfish—frozen balls can be used. As soon as you hook the first fish, drop the balls overboard until the entire school is following the boat. The fish will hit the rigged baits or lures offered them.

Whole, small fish such as pilchards or glass minnows can also be used as chum and are dispensed a little at a time into the water. Some fishermen use live fish and stun them by hitting the fish against the boat before putting them in the water.

Netting and Gaffing

After hooking a fish, you must get it into the boat or release it alive. Always release fish that aren't going to be eaten. For most fish a large pliers will be a good release tool: grab the hook shank with the pliers and twist the hook out of the fish's mouth. Do not take the fish out of the water. Fish properly released will be back for more sport soon. If you are fishing only for sport, use a barbless hook; the barbless hook is easy to release and does not do as much damage to the fish.

If the fish is to going to be eaten, decide between a landing net and a gaff. Your choice will depend on the size of the fish. You can net any fish of less than 15 pounds; larger fish will be handled more easily with a gaff.

Get a net ready while the fish is being fought, before it is brought to the boat. The fisherman should not tighten the drag, but rather should keep the rod tip high in the air to absorb the shock if the fish tries a final lunge. Now quickly position the net in front of the fish. In one motion net the fish head first and lift the net and fish into the boat. Don't try to net from the tail of the fish, if the fish panics and bolts you will miss him. Netting head first forces the fish, if he runs, to run into the net.

If the fish is too large to net, get the gaff ready. The angler should keep the rod tip as high as he can. The gaffer will have a glove on one hand and the gaff in the other. Put the gaff into the water and, with the gloved hand, grab the leader and bring the point of the gaff up quickly into the center belly of the fish. Lift with both the leader and the gaff to boat the fish.

Transporting Frozen Bait

Have a small cooler reserved for bait. The cooler should have a frozen bottle or gel pack to keep the bait cold. Before you start the trip, pack the bait cooler with all the cut bait, whole rigged baits, and chum you may need. As you leave the dock open the first packs of bait you plan to use, and let those baits thaw. Keep thawing more baits as you fish. At the end of the trip return baits in good condition to the cooler, and freeze them when you get home. The baits will be ready for the next fishing trip.

Going Fishing

One of the wonderful surprising pleasures of saltwater fishing is that you don't even have to have a boat. You can fish from shores and banks, piers, bridges, canals, jetties and on flats. The general techniques are similar, but each kind of fishing also has its peculiarities.

Fishing from Jetties and Banks

In most cases you will be fishing from rocky shorelines. The primary catches will be black drum, bluefish, redfish, jacks, sea trout, striped bass, and even some flounder. Use medium tackle, about 20- to 30-

pound test gear. Cast just over the rocks with live or frozen shrimp, jigs or spoons, or any cut bait. The fish will try to run with the bait into the overgrown barnacle-covered rocks cutting your monofilament. The heavier rigs will allow you to keep the fish from the rocks. This method of fishing can be very productive once you get to know the territory. Some fishermen prefer to fish alone, and others like company. When learning a new area, get help if you can. You can fish jetties and banks anytime, but be certain that you keep records of the time and tide conditions. This record will soon show you the most productive conditions for fishing a certain area.

Good equipment for this type of fishing is either a stout spinning rig or a stout baitcasting rig. A long handled net is also necessary.

Fishing from the Shore

When fishing from a beach or gravel-like shoreline, the method is surf casting and mackerel, snook, tarpon, bluefish, stripers, and occasionally groupers and snappers are the game. This is a quiet and contemplative type of fishing, done alone or with friends. Surf casting can be done either night or day, normally with an eight-foot-long spinning rod and large capacity reel.

Fishing from Piers or Bridges

You can cast, bottom fish or let your bait drift in the tide. The bridges and piers are always hot fishing grounds, maybe because the basic food chain starts with the marine organisms attached to the pilings and rocks of the bridge or maybe because the active fishing assures the fish of a continuing food source. Whatever the reason, bridge and pier fishing is productive. You must make a choice between roaming the length of the bridge or pier, or fishing from one or two positions. Both methods are effective, and both have advantages.

The fisherman who roams from one end to the other covers more fishing ground. He will do a lot of casting and use several lures and baits. He will investigate several spots in order to locate some fish over a grassy spot or in a hole. The amount of gear you can carry is limited. The one-favorite-spot fisherman will have borrowed his wife's shopping cart or his neighbor's little wagon, may have a chair and an umbrella, a crony or two nearby. He probably fishes at least two rigs on the bottom or swaying in the tidal flow. He will be waiting for a school of moving fish, or the hungry predator on the prowl. Feeding fish move around.

Both types of fishing catch fish, and the fish will be snook, sea trout, mackerel, snapper, grunt, and on piers even grouper and sailfish.

Pier fishing is not as inactive as this angler makes it look, but it does have its relaxing moments.

Fishing from a pier can also produce cobia, kingfish and pompano. Fishing can be done night or day. Most pier and bridge rigs are in the 30-pound test class or heavier. Cutoffs on barnacles and rocks are a problem unless you control the fish and bring it in quickly.

You can use baitcasting rigs, spinning tackle, or even a boat rod and reel. You must have a light-weight and easy-to-carry bridge gaff, which will enable you to gaff a fish 60 feet or more below.

Flats Fishing

Start fishing the flats with a chart, and if you are going to use a boat, a depth finder. Study the areas you are going to fish. Look for holes, patch reefs and the channels. You must know where you are going, but more important, how to get there. The only way to learn this is by studying the chart; unfortunately the area you want to fish could change, and so could the features that will be your guide to the area.

Know where you are trying to go. After studying the area you want to fish, go to a nearby shore and start walking across the flat. Be careful of holes. Remember that you must carry all the gear you will need until you return to shore. You are fishing for bonefish, permit, and as a bonus, sharks. A shark on light tackle on the flats can be a real handful! Patch reefs can be very productive, and will yield snapper and sea trout.

Flats fishing requires light or even ultra-light spinning tackle, light baitcasting tackle, or a saltwater flyfishing rig. This is mostly sport fishing so you will release all of your catch, therefore you don't need to carry a net.

Canals and Inlets

Almost any type of fishing can be done from canal banks. Cane poles may be as effective as a fly rod. The canals feature snook, tarpon, jacks, and small snappers. Before you take a fish for eating, look carefully around your fishing spot. Most canals and inlets are heavily polluted with fertilizers and insecticides, from lawns, gardens and farms. If the canal or inlet is in an unpopulated area, the catch is probably safe to eat.

The Party Boats

These boats are 40 to 90 feet long, and are called head boats, drift boats, or party boats. They fish anchored or drifting; they fish all day, 8:00 AM until noon, 1:00 PM until 5:00 PM and late evening. Some fish on trips up to 7 days, and some even troll. All party boats have some traits in common—they catch fish, they are inexpensive, they catch exceptional varieties of fish, they are safe, and they offer an extremely convenient successful saltwater fishing experience.

Picking Your Pleasure. Find out the details of the fishing trip before you go along, so that you won't be disappointed if the fishing trip does not match your expectations. First consider the time schedule. The boat will depart and return based on its schedule, and not on your wishes. Fishing either day or night can be productive. Daytime fishing will produce more yellowtail, dolphin, wahoo, cobia and sailfish. Night time will yield more king mackerel and groupers. Sharks, snappers and tunas are caught at any time. Grunts are where you find them. Night time is cooler but night is harder fishing because tangled lines are a surety on party boats and very difficult to clear in the lower visibility of night time. With the exception of weekends and holidays, daytime trips are usually less crowded than evening trips. The time that is most convenient for you should be the overriding consideration. If you are taking children out for the first time, probably a daytime trip will be more successful.

Picking Your Boat. There are three major considerations: the boat, the skipper, and the crew. The boat should be clean and seaworthy, and sturdy enough to handle the type of seas you will be fishing. Since you will be out for several hours, the boat should have a clean useable head (marine toilet). Some boats will sell soft drinks, candy bars and even sandwiches. You should decide if you will buy them from the boat or bring your own. It should be permissible for you to bring your own cooler, both for snacks and for carrying your fish home.

You can learn the policies of the boat by asking before you pay for the trip. One question is whether the crew will be available to help you and the other anglers or is the crew going to fish. Avoid boats where the skipper permits the crew to fish. Also make certain that what you catch is yours to take with you. This is not as big a problem on party boats as it is on charter boats, but be sure you know the answer before you sign on.

Another, and preferred, way to find out about a boat is to be on hand when the boat returns from a trip. You can see the type of fish caught, and ask the departing fishermen what the trip was like. Sometimes even after a trip is skunked the anglers will. praise the skipper for trying.

The skipper is key to a pleasant outing. A good captain will make certain that all the fishermen have a good time. Some skippers will keep trying for game fish even when it appears hopeless, others will try to keep you happy by finding at least a grunt hole. Both types of skippers are right, which would you prefer? Unfortunately, there are bad as well good fishing captains. The good captain will have the skill to find the fish, the discipline to keep the crew trying and the occasional misbehaving customer in line, and the ability to keep the fishermen happy on good days and bad.

MIKE ARTHUR

A wide variety of fishes can be caught while fishing from a party boat. While not typical of party-boat catches, this spearfish was a real surprise and a bonus fish caught on a party boat.

You will have more contact with the crew than with the skipper, therefore the crew will have more to do with your fishing day. Some crews are off the street casual workers who know less about fishing than the greenest customer; others are pleasant trained professionals who are working to become captains themselves. A good crew will help you get started, tell you how to catch more fish, mark the fish you catch to avoid a later dispute, tell you to get your lines in when necessary, clear all tangles, and the best will, for a tip, clean your catch.

Now you have selected a trip. The boat will run out to the first fishing hole. If you picked a drift boat it will shift into neutral and drift with the current, the crew will assign you a spot, or you will position yourself on the rail ready to fish. Someone in the bow will start chumming, and you want to secure a position that puts your bait in the drift of the chum. Put your line in and you are fishing.

If the boat anchors, the regulars will have taken all the spots at the stern. The chum will drift from the bow to the stern so the best spots are at or very near the stern rail. A good captain and crew will give everyone a chance at the best spots. During the day you will soon see a flash of color in the water and soon everyone will be boating fish. Your baits may drift for yellowtail or gamefish, others will fish deep for king mackerel, snapper or grouper.

No equipment is needed for party boat fishing, the boat will supply rods and reels, terminal tackle, and bait. Some anglers will bring their own rods and tackle boxes. If you bring your own rod and reel, bring at least a 12-pound test rig, or better yet, a 20-pound test rig. The heavy gear is needed to gain control of your fish immediately. If you don't control the fish, you will be responsible for many tangles and you will lose most of your fish in the rocks below.

It is hard to imagine a more chaotic situation than an almost full party boat in a large school of yellowtail or dolphin. What fun!

All you need is a few dollars, a little time, a good boat, a good skipper and a friendly crew for a fun-filled day of saltwater fishing.

Small Boat Fishing, Inshore

Saltwater fishing in a small boat increases the angler's fishing territory. Now fishing is possible in the bays, inlets, and canals well beyond the shoreline. A small boat can be as small as 12-feet or up to 18-feet long. The larger boats offer increased versatility, comfort, safety and convenience. The types of inshore fishing available are varied. You can fish patch reefs and holes of the bays, and drop offs of canals and bays. A boat as small as a john boat can fish these waters, but the instability of this design can cause problems unless extreme care is taken in any movement around the boat. This is not bass fishing! These waters can produce 20-pound snook, 60- to 100-pound tarpon, and even larger sharks. If your choice is a john boat, stick to the canals and the shallow bays and fish for redfish and snapper.

A 14-foot bass boat can serve as a good fishing platform in the inshore waters. Their speed and elevated fishing chairs will be useful. Stability may be a problem, but is increased by a wide beam.

The ideal inshore fishing, sometimes called "back country", boat is 16 or 18 feet long with a 7 foot beam, has a slight deep vee in the stern, shallow draft, and is almost free of hardware. Even low bow rails will get in your way when fishing, and cleats on the deck or gunwale will add a tripping hazard. Required navigational lights are essential since you will be doing some night fishing for grouper and snook. A side console, steering and control station, is desirable so the center line of the boat is available for fore and aft traffic. A starboard console is desirable so that the weight of the skipper can counteract the torque created by a single outboard motor.

JACK ZINZOW

This catch is the result of a good day back-country fishing. Among the snook and redfish are a sea trout and crevalle jack.

Cero mackerel are caught by bottom fishing over patch reefs or in inlets.

A compromise, an excellent one, is an 18 foot center console deep vee which can double as an offshore boat. This boat will have restricted use in the shallow water areas of inshore fishing. Thin water is a constant problem for the inshore fisherman. If the boat skims across the flats on a full plane it will draw the least water, but when a shallow spot is hit the boat will go hard aground. In this situation you may have to wait for the incoming tide even if you get out of the boat and try pushing. Or hitting an oyster bar can destroy the boat and cause injury.

Knowledge of the navigational charts and the tide tables is required to fish inshore waters. Caution is essential until you know the waters you are fishing much better than you know the back of your hand. In all saltwater fishing areas someone will publish local monthly tide tables. Always have one on board and never leave the dock without checking the tables. At best, ignorance of the tidal conditions will result in a waste of time. You must also know that high or low tide are relative terms. Sometimes a low will be only 1.1 feet below "mean low water", at other times in the same spot low will be almost 4 feet below mean low water. So you must know both the time and the scope of the tides.

Small Offshore Boats

There was a time when the center console open fisherman was considered a "poor man's" sportfisherman. However these 20- to 26-foot boats now range in price from $20,000 for a basic boat, motor and trailer to $100,000 for a fully rigged and full featured 26 footer.

These crafts are for offshore work. Normally equipped with two radios, two engines, and a compass, they also carry all required safety equipment. They are built for speed and safety rather than comfort. Many have leaning bars instead of seats, so you must stand for the whole fishing trip. All of these boats have insulated fish boxes and rod holders in every available spot.

Of all the equipment the main propulsion engine is the most important. It can be diesel but, due to the heavy weight of a diesel engine, gasoline engines are normal for boats of this size. The engine can be an outboard, an inboard, or the combination of an inboard engine with an outdrive. All types have advantages, the inboard and the inboard/outboard (I/O) offer fuel economy but use up a large amount of the space available in a boat of this size. The pure outboard is easy to replace and uses a minimum of fishing space. Any good propulsion system will do, but a fishing boat of this type should reach a plane at about 20 to 24 miles per hour, and run easily at 40 miles per hour.

BOB STEARNS

Small offshore boats let the angler fish anywhere he wants to go and get there fast. The grouper's not bad either.

However, a boat with one engine is a serious risk when out of sight of land. A second small engine, a "kicker", can be added to any boat of this type. The kicker should be large enough to push the boat at a minimum of 5 miles per hour. This isn't racing, but this speed will get you home. Most kickers aren't run often enough. If you have one get in the habit of using it. In many situations you can troll with a kicker. Some anglers claim they get improved fuel economy by trolling with a kicker, and some claim they get more fish. In any case two, or more, engines are better than one. Twin main engines are fine.

Never go offshore without a good functioning radio. Again two are better, but be certain that your radio is in prime shape by making frequent transmission checks.

There are many items of optional equipment that will improve your fishing efficiency. Foremost is the set of outriggers. The outriggers permit the use of more baits and let you vary the presentation of the baits. When trolling it is most effective to fish five or more baits plus a teaser. This gives the appearance of a school of baitfish. For this type of boat, outriggers are standard at 15 feet, but they can be longer or shorter to fit the boat. If the outriggers when laid on the deck extend more than 3 feet beyond the transom they can be broken easily when maneuvering the boat or the trailer. If that is the case, trim them to fit the boat before you rig them. Even a pair of 12-foot outriggers will give you a fishing span of about 32 feet, enough for 5 lines and a teaser.

Another excellent device is the downrigger. It adds another dimension to your fishing area. With practice you can run two lines off a single downrigger. Fishing with a downrigger requires a lot of effort but it will catch fish when nothing else seems to work.

An alternative to the downrigger is a wire line with a heavy weight and an electric reel. This will accomplish the same goal of getting your baits down to where the fish are, but reeling a fish in by pushing a button is not much sport no matter how effective it is.

While this gear is primarily for trolling, there is other equipment that is very helpful for finding bottom fish. LORAN is available today at a reasonable price and will help you locate a particular fishing spot with an accuracy of about 3 feet. This means that you can always get back to a productive hole or wreck. Many charts and texts are written locating the wrecks and reefs in any given area and the LORAN co-ordinates are given. Of course LORAN is a superb navigational device and should be part of the equipment on a boat that regularly goes offshore, but don't ignore its fish-finding capabilities.

Many depth finders are now called fish finders. The new sophisticated depth finders will highlight fish in a different color or display a fish silhouette, not only indicating the size of the fish, but some even let you select the size of fish, and the depth finder will ignore fish smaller or larger than you are looking for.

A speedometer is useful in trimming your boat to maximum fuel efficiency; if you decide to install one get one with an odometer. The odometer is a useful navigating device, but also excellent for locating, or relocating, fishing wrecks and fishing holes.

One device you should have that is not intended for fish finding, but for the safety of your party is an EPIRB. This stands for an electronic position indicating radio beacon. Hopefully, you will never need it, but if you do it can save your life. When you activate this beacon it sends a recognized distress signal that allows a rescuer to locate your boat, or what is left of it, quickly. If you can afford an offshore boat, you should be able to afford one of these easily available safety devices.

The Sportfisherman

These boats range from 26 feet to 60 feet in length, and cost up to $500,000, but the cost can double depending on the luxury requirements of the buyer. Most of us won't own one of these, but if you are in the market for a sportfisherman, hire a marine architect.

Charterboats. Most anglers will get their experience with sportfishing boats on a charter boat. The cost of a half- or full-day charter varies

SANDRA ROMASHKO

The mate struggles with a sailfish caught on a 12-pound test spinning rig aboard a chartered sportfisherman.

from dock to dock, and with the demand for trips and the price of fuel. Since most boats will fish up to six anglers you can get a full-day charter for about $100 per day per angler for a full boat. Many captains will arrange to fill out your charter with other anglers, but then you will spend seven hours in a small area with strangers. Maybe you will get lucky and have fine companions, but who knows.

When you are preparing to go on a chartered fishing trip there are many questions to be answered before you are committed. Be certain you get these matters resolved before you leave the dock.

First go see the boat and meet the captain. Look at his boat, the head, and his fishing gear. Check his electronics. Try to meet him when he is just in from a charter, then you can see his catch and check the mood of his departing party. Probably 90% of the fishing captains are helpful, personable and pleasant, but not all are. Having decided that he and his gear may make for a pleasant day, there are still many questions to be resolved.

First find out what your responsibilities are. In many areas the fishing party is expected to furnish soft drinks and lunch for themselves and the crew. Check with the skipper before bringing beer on board, but normally beer won't be a problem; hard liquor may be a serious problem. Assume the captain will furnish the rods and reels, but ask about gear, and discuss what kind of fish you want to catch. Find out if the captain accepts credit cards, a check or only cash. Ask what kind of baits he will supply. In recent years some captains have a standard contract that you may or may not see. Ask if he has such a standard contract and if he has, read it, and if it is acceptable, sign it. If it is not acceptable, change it or leave. You are the customer, and your desires should prevail.

Now we come to tougher questions. Some captains have decided that selling the catch is a regular source of income for the boat. Get a firm agreement beforehand on who owns the fish that are caught on your trip. You might want to agree to an arrangement that the angling party gets several pounds of cleaned fillets, and the boat keeps the rest. Frequently the captain will agree that all the fish you want are yours.

Another question to be resolved is who cleans the fish. Most of the time the mate will clean the fish in return for a $10 or $20 tip, depending on the number of fish. If there are a lot of fish, it may be best for the fishermen to pitch in and help rather than wait for the mate to clean all the fish.

Icing the catch should never be a problem, but sometimes it is. Beautiful catches of hundreds of pounds of prime edible fish have been ruined by captains saving $3 on ice. Some will even argue with you when you question the amount of ice being used. Insist that the fish are heavily iced.

You may have to deal with the tricky question of mounting your catch. Normally this question doesn't come up until you have just brought a magnificent sailfish into the boat, you are flushed with the pleasure of your catch and the captain and crew try to persuade you to mount that beautiful catch. To understand what is going on you must know the mechanics of taxidermy. Most, or all in some areas, of the captains are agents for one taxidermy firm. If the boat had a standard contract, the contract probably stated that the captain would have the right to determine who mounted your catch. If you agree to have it mounted you will have to pay a fee when you get back to the dock that will be about 50% of the total cost of the mount. Frequently this 50% fee is the agent's commission. The captain and crew pocket this fee, and call the taxidermist to pick up your fish. Later, maybe six months later, you will be contacted to pay the balance so the taxidermist can finish the mount and ship it to you. So what do you get for you money? Many mounts are 100% painted fiberglass and plastic. Your $800 has been split about $400 to the agent captain and $400 to the taxidermist. Not all deals must be like this. If you want a mount, you can demand that you have the right to pick the taxidermist. In most markets there are taxidermists who will deal directly with you, pick up the fish and mount the $800 fish for less than $600, and guarantee that your mount will contain the fins, bill and lower jaw from your fish!

What this all simply means is that because of the money involved you must know what the terms of your charter are every time you go on a charter boat; most captains are anxious to please you.

Trolling

This is a very good method for catching a wide variety of fish. Trolling with four or five lines on or near the surface is a good way to catch marlin or dolphin. (This dolphin is a fish and is not to be confused with the mammal that is also called dolphin.) There are several methods of trolling. Very slow trolling can be effective with live bait. You must not drown the baitfish. In the section on live baits several methods of rigging baitfish are discussed. Trolling at 5 to 10 knots is the most common trolling speed, usually with artificial lures or with rigged dead baits. High speed trolling is done only with artificial lures. Slow trolling with live bait in 90 to 120 feet of water is a good system for catching sailfish. Slow trolling with live bait and a downrigger in 60 to 90 feet is the most productive when fishing for king mackerel.

Mid-speed trolling with a mix of rigged dead baits, some skirted some not, and artificial lures is effective for finding dolphin. And sometimes you will find marlin, or yellowfin tuna.

High speed trolling is the preferred method for marlin since you can cover a lot of ocean in a few hours.

Trolling large artificial lures at high speed covers a large amount of ocean in search of the blue marlin.

Remember the idea of trolling is to present the bait naturally so that it looks like normal prey to the gamefish. Though it is not fully understood why, most small bait-sized fish gather in schools of dozens or even hundreds of fish. Therefore you want to present your baits as a school of fish. Trolling two baits behind the boat does not excite the fish. Add outriggers and troll five or seven lines plus a teaser and you appear to offer a school of fish. The teaser is designed to attract gamefish, but not to catch them. Some skippers refuse to "drag anything behind the boat that doesn't have a hook in it". Unless you like to buy large expensive teasers and lose the teasers to sharp-toothed fish, forget the hook. If you are fly fishing for sailfish or other large offshore gamefish, you use a teaser of live baitfish, dead baitfish, or an artificial lure to get the fish excited and then offer the fly. This technique works as well with spinning or casting rigs, but when trolling place your first baitfish about five feet behind the teaser, and spread the other baits to either side and behind the leading teaser.

The type of rigs and terminal tackle you use when trolling is also important. Successful trolling requires having a variety of types of baits and a variety of colors available. You must offer variety! Carrying many fully-rigged lures poses some problems, but it is essential to have the rigs on the leaders before you leave the dock. When trolling it is acceptable to have some hardware on the terminal tackle. Therefore, you can put a snap swivel on the double line. The leader of a rig can have either a swivel or a loop knot to attach to the snap swivel on your line. If you rig with a wire leader, start the leader with a loop made with a haywire twist; if you rig with Steelon (plastic coated braided steel) you can make a loop using a connector sleeve and crimp. If you rig with a monofilament leader, tie a loop knot.

Determine the material and length of the leader by the type of fish you are after. For billfish a wire or Steelon leader of about six feet is necessary. For big toothy fish like kingfish, barracuda, or bluefish, three feet of wire or Steelon are necessary. For most other species, you can use three feet of monofilament for the leader.

Lures with treble hooks are a difficult storage problem. To avoid tangles use the plastic box the lure came in or buy small boxes to fit the lures. However most lures with either a single hook or double hooks can be stored in a small plastic bag with a zipper-type closure. Simply coil the leader and slip the lure and leader into the bag. When stored in a bag of moderately heavy plastic (freezer-weight bags) the lures will not tangle and will be ready for serious fishing. Slip the selected lure from its see-through bag, uncoil it, and snap it on your line and you are ready!

Use this same trick for your leaders with bare hooks that will be used for cut bait. Tie on a single hook or snell on up to four hooks, tie a loop knot on three to six feet of monofilament leader with a loop knot on the other end. Cut a piece of corrugated board 1/2 inch smaller than the plastic bag. Cut four or five slits about a 1/4 inch long on both ends of the board, push the hook into one edge of the board, wrap the leader around the board into the slits, label the size of the hooks and insert into the bag. This method of storing your hooks makes them available immediately when you need them and the leader won't be tangled.

Casting

Casting with either spinning tackle or fly tackle, or bait casting is an excellent way to catch trout or many other species.

All systems of casting produce the same results—you can fly, bait or spin cast for dolphin, tarpon, snook, sailfish, sea trout, wahoo, cobia or any fish you can see. If you can catch it casting, any technique will do.

One major difference between fly casting and the other methods is that the fly is tied directly to the leader that is tied to the tippet, which is tied to the to the weighted fly line. The tippet is a piece of monofilament that determines the weight class you are fishing. If the tippet is 8 pound-test line, then the fishing class is 8 pound. For spinning or bait casting the bait is tied to the leader and the leader is tied to the monofilament line on your reel. So instead of having a few inches of test line, you have 350 yards of test line.

Deep Trolling

Most of the fish in the ocean are not sitting on the surface waiting for you to drag a bait past them. Most of the fish are below the surface, some as far down as 600 to 800 feet. Getting your bait down to them is a problem with several solutions.

Deep trolling can be accomplished through several techniques. The simplest method is the use of lead weights on your line, but trolling at speeds of more than four knots will lift a weight causing it to come up to the surface. If you use enough weight to take your lure down 20 or 30 feet you will tire just holding the rod, and you probably will not have enough strength to actually fight a fish.

Wire line is one moderately expensive alternative. There are many types of weighted line. Multi-strand wire is available and easy to use. It doesn't take your lure very deep, and most experienced anglers won't use it because if one strand breaks the line is weakened and the broken strand can cut your hand. Solid wire line is available in stainless steel or Monel. Stainless wire is four times the cost of monofilament and Monel is seven times the cost of monofilament. A wire line rig must be set up and used only for wire line. A medium to heavy rod with ceramic guides and a wide shallow revolving spool reel is required. Fifty-pound test Monel wire is the most commonly used and special reels are made for wire. Avoid any kinks in the metal as these are certain to break the wire under strain. Without added weight in the form of torpedo shaped sinkers the wire will take a bait down at about 10 feet for each 100 feet of wire if the boat is trolling at about 5 mph. Slower speeds will let the bait run deeper, and the shape of some lures will add some additional depth. Wire is not easy to use: be careful to avoid snarls that will cause kinks, and don't snag the bottom. If the wire is tied directly to the bait, the actions of the hooked fish are transmitted directly to the arms and shoulders of the angler, causing fatigue to the fisherman. Therefore, a monofilament leader is used between the wire and the wire leader used as terminal tackle. Also a rod with a very flexible tip and stiff butt will help. The serious meat fisherman may use an electric reel, available at most tackle shops.

Deep diving plugs are also an alternative for getting down to where the fish are. There is no way to control these plugs in any range of depth in the water. This is an inexpensive, but not very effective method of fishing deep. If a deep diving plug is all you have, by all means use one.

Planers of all shapes and colors are available. The concept here is that the planer dives taking your action lure, connected by a long leader, down with it. Again control of depth is a problem. When a fish hits your lure the planer will trip thereby minimizing its resistance to your fight with the fish. However, the planer is there and you will feel

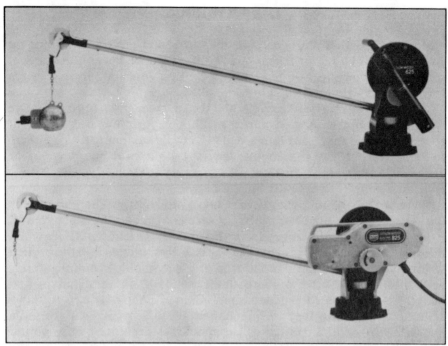

Downriggers provide the most effective way of getting your baits down deep while trolling. They are available in manual (top) or electric (bottom) styles of retrieving the weight.

it. Also the planers have a tendency to trip themselves, after which the planer must be retrieved and reset.

The most expensive and most effective means of getting deep is a downrigger. A downrigger is also the most work, but fishing effectively requires effort. The downrigger acts just like an outrigger. You lower the downrigger weight on a stainless cable by a large gunwale-mounted reel. The weight is shaped to avoid twisting during trolling. As the line runs down you attach a fishing line to a release clip on the cable. Usually two lines are attached and fished at about 30 feet and 60 feet down. The release clip will hold the fishing line until a fish strikes. When a fish hits, the fishing line is released and you fight the fish on your tackle without any incumbering weight. This is very effective but a lot of practice is needed. A manual downrigger (you retrieve the weight by cranking) can be purchased for about $200, but the electric model ready to go will be close to $500. Lost weights—you will lose some—cost $15 to $30 each.

Fishing deep is more expensive and harder than dragging baits along the surface, but deep trolling is maybe the most effective means of fishing. The advantage is that you can fish at any desired depth with any light tackle you want.

Bottom Fishing

Among the best eating fish in the world are flounders, groupers, snappers and yellowtail. Among the best fighting fish in the world are amberjack, or any of the jack family. The kingfish is both, good eating and good fighting. All of these fish are taken by some form of bottom fishing. Bottom fishing is more work and not nearly as much fun as trolling, but it can be so productive.

It's simple—anchor the boat over a hole, wreck, or reef and drop weighted rigs with cut bait over the side. Wait a while and you will have a cooler full of fish. The cut bait can be mullet, mullet heads (a treat for grouper), ballyhoo, squid or any other cut fish. Always use some form of chum. Anchor, drop your baits, and chum. Wait for the chum to work, about 30 minutes. If you don't get a hit, move to another spot. A depth finder and LORAN are important to this type of fishing, but if you haven't invested in LORAN use distance, ranges and shore markers to position yourself accurately over a proven spot.

Another method is to deep jig. This is a strenuous activity. You drop your weighted bait to the bottom and retrieve the line in a continuous series of jerks made by rapidly lifting the rod tip and reeling in the slack line as you drop the tip, then repeat.

Both methods of bottom fishing require that you find a productive spot and properly weight your bait. Your bait should have enough

BOB GOBEN

Amberjack are terrific fighting fish which can be caught bottom fishing over wrecks with cut bait.

These grouper were caught offshore by bottom fishing with cut bait over holes in the Gulf of Mexico. Large amberjack are mixed with the grouper catch.

The artificial reef program is providing fishing areas easily accessible to fishermen. Derelict ships like the one above are sunk and within a short period of time become covered with marine growth which attracts food and game fishes and become fertile fishing grounds.

weight added to take the bait to the bottom with your line pulled almost vertical. When you reach bottom (your line will go slack) retrieve the bait to about 18-24 inches above bottom. If you use too little weight, you will need 300 feet of line to reach bottom in 80 feet of water; too much weight and you won't feel the strikes and you will work harder retrieving your bait. In either situation you will lose most of the fish.

Live baits are also very effective bottom fishing. Almost any small live fish will do. The sinker should be tied to the line below the bait. A spreader device, either purchased or home made from wire, such as a coat hanger, should be used to keep the bait from entangling with the fishing line.

There are groups, political and civic, that sink artificial reefs in all saltwater fishing areas. Commonly called artificial reefs, these wrecks of ships and other debris such as huge mounds of tires are really fish habitats. After they are submerged, coral and other marine growth cover the debris and these reefs attract small fish that attract larger fish. This is a very successful program and as a serious fisherman you should know where these artificial reefs are. Charts are published with the location and LORAN readings of the reefs. Bottom fishing is productive over reefs, but be sure to lift your bait off the bottom after you have reached bottom.

Bottom fishing, especially deep jigging, also can produce sailfish and dolphin as a bonus, but you can expect to catch snappers, groupers, mackerel among a great variety of reef fish.

The Fish

These are only some of the fish you can catch in salt water, but they are the most common or most sought after.

Amberjack *(Seriola dumerili)* are usually found over wrecks and artificial reefs. Use bottom fishing techniques with cut bait or jigs tipped with cut bait.

Barracuda *(Sphyraena barracuda)* are caught incidentally with almost any fishing method, but if you are hunting barracuda troll around cuts or jetties. If you cast for a barracuda you have spotted, don't cast closer than 10 feet in front of the fish and use a fast, uneven retrieve. Barracuda prefer spoons or jigs tipped with dead baitfish. Yellow is a favored color.

Black drum *(Pogonias cromis)*, also called drum, will be caught from breakwaters, jetties, in the surf, and around mangrove sloughs. You can bottom fish for them or cast shrimp, cut bait, spoons or jigs.

Bluefin tuna *(Thunnus thynnus)* are by far the largest of the tunas. They are found migrating in schools of a few to a dozen large fish. They are fished by drifting or trolling large live or dead baits such as squid, mullet, and mackerel.

BOB GOBEN

Amberjack can be found anywhere in salt water but they often congregate over high relief rock or coral bottom and around wrecks or buoys.

Cobia usually occur singly or in small groups and are often around wrecks, buoys and floating debris, and about large sea animals such as rays and turtles.

Bluefish *(Pomatomus saltarix)* travel in voracious schools and will hit a cast cut bait, a plug, a spoon or a jig.

Blue marlin *(Makaira nigricans)* are one of the premier gamefish. Most will be caught high-speed or moderate-speed trolling with artificial baits, but some will be boated by anglers fishing live bait by dropping an 8/0 hook beneath a school of dolphin. Since you are fishing for big fish, use a big lure. Others will be found under fishing frigate birds. The trick is to find the fish.

Bonefish *(Albula spp.)* are one of the few fish that must first be seen before you can catch them. You will find them by spotting their tails as they feed in as little as eight inches of water. Approach them either wading or by quietly polling your boat within casting distance. Catch them with a cast just in front of the feeding fish with either a fly rod or a spinning rod. Shrimp or shrimp-like flies are the primary baits, but also used are small crabs and squid, or pieces of clam or conch. Be ready for a long run at high speed if you hook a bonefish.

Cobia *(Rachycentron canadum)* hit hard, run and jump. They are found inshore along beaches and inlets; offshore around deep reefs, wrecks and buoys, and under large rays and whales. You will catch them trolling, bottom fishing, deep jigging and casting. The preferred baits are live fish, cut bait and strip baits.

Dolphin *(Coryphaena hippurus)* are found by spotting a likely spot for fishing for them. Signs are: any floating debris, floating weed patches, feeding birds, or a rip current. Keep a sharp lookout for any such sign, approach the area with moderate care and be ready to fish. First troll around the area, any good weed patch is worth twice around. Alternatively, you can just get to the patch, current or birds, and chum. You probably won't keep up with a rip or with birds, and a good sized weed patch will be too large for one-spot chumming to work. After you get the first hit you will have to fight two urges, the first is to slow or stop the boat, don't. Keep the boat moving until you have at least the second fish on a line. The other urge will be to bring the first hooked fish into the boat. Just lead him close to the boat, 40 to 60 feet. If you have brought up a school of dolphin, you should see them. With the second fish securely hooked, bring in the first fish. If the fish are a size you like and you have a school up, throw in a little chum and get casting! You must always keep one fish in the water or you will lose the school. One way to do this and let your party enjoy fishing is to use a Moody rig. This is 30 feet of 20-pound test line with about a one ounce sinker and a baited #4 hook. As the boat is slowing, but still moving, throw the baited hook in the water and secure the inboard end on a convenient cleat. As soon as you have a fish on the Moody rig everyone can cast, catch and land their fish, confident you will not lose the school prematurely. Don't get carried away, never land any fish unless you know who is going to eat that fish.

Some days you will not be able to find any visible place to fish. Then your only choice is to fish the open ocean. Don't give up! Many fine catches are made during days of dragging baits through the open water. The biggest dolphin do not travel in schools, but normally there will be a large bull dolphin and one or two large cows roaming the ocean together as pelagic predators. Other challenging fish are also roaming the ocean. You may hit a school of great fighting yellowfin tuna. Your first hint will be simultaneous strikes on several trolled baits, followed by a shoulder wrenching fight. Or you will you will cross the path of a foraging white or blue marlin.

Flounder (all species) live on muddy, sandy or gravel bottoms. Chum and fish on the bottom with cut squid, cut mullet, clams and worms for bait. Drifting will keep the baits moving and cover a lot of fishing grounds.

Groupers (all species) are excellent food fish. You will catch grouper bottom fishing from an anchored or drifting boat. The preferred baits are mullet heads, cut fish, strip baits, bucktails, spoons and jigs. Fine catches are also made deep trolling.

King Mackerel (Scomberomorus cavalla), also called kingfish, is caught by moderate-speed deep trolling. The problem is getting the baits down to where the fish are. The technique of deep trolling is discussed on page 51. An alternative is to drift slowly with the baits deep, or to anchor and chum in 60 to 90 feet of water. In any case use

Barracuda are pelagic and migratory fish and can be caught just about anywhere. Grouper are found on smooth sand or mud bottoms but will frequent wrecks or high relief bottom of coral and rocks.

a feathered jig with three hooks and a ballyhoo skewered securely on the three hooks; sometimes large live shrimp will do. Kingfish are notorious short hitters, that is, they will take just the back half of your bait. Be certain there is a hook near the tail to catch him.

Permit *(Trachinotus falcatus)* are found on banks and shallows. You can cast for them, or bottom fish. Amphipods called sand fleas and a small crab are the preferred baits, but shrimp, clams, conch and jigs are also effective.

Redfish *(Sciaenops ocellata)*, also known as red drum and channel bass, are hooked casting shrimp, jigs, cut bait, or jigs tipped with shrimp or cut bait. Fish around inlets and shellfish beds, and red mangrove sloughs.

Sailfish *(Istiophorus platypterus)*. Effective fishing for sailfish demands specific techniques. Slow trolling or drifting with live baits is

59

effective. Most effective is live baits held at the surface with a kite. Special fishing kites are sold for this purpose, but any good flying kite will do; a parafoil kite works very well. The kite should be flown from a stout rod with any 20-pound level-wind reel. Twenty pound line is strong enough to fly the kite. Attach about 60 feet of leader to the kite with a swivel on the kite, then a three way swivel 35 feet from the kite rig. Attach another three way swivel 20 feet farther and finish off the leader with about five feet of leader and a swivel. Attach another line of about 20 feet ending with a clothespin from each three way swivel. American made spring loaded wooden clothespins are inexpensive and made with stainless steel springs. As the kite is flown attach the fishing line by a #4 snap clip so the clip is held in the jaws of the clothespin, and the fishing line can run freely through the clip. Continue flying the kite, when you come to the next clothespin attach a second fishing line in the same way. The kite will fly downwind away from the live baits you are drifting behind the boat. With a little practice you can lengthen or shorten the fishing lines so the live bait on the kite rig is always splashing just at the surface of the water. This attracts fish—including sharks. As the sharks approach the bait you can briefly lift the bait out of the water, so the shark will not be able to take your bait.

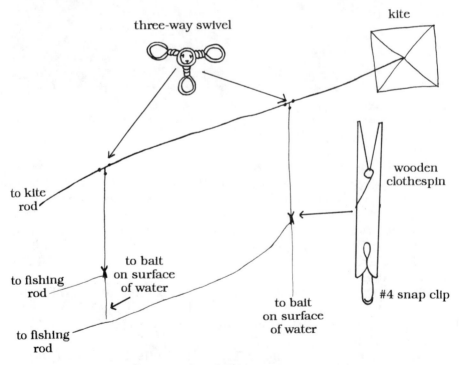

kite fishing rig

Sea Trout (*Cynoscion nebulosus*). Trolling at 5-6 mph can be very effective in finding sea trout over grassy flats. Simply troll a small jig tipped with a piece of fresh or frozen shrimp over the flat until you catch a trout. Then carefully note your position, go up wind 50 or 60 feet, drop your anchor and cast either a shrimp-tipped jig or a live shrimp. Trout, and some other fish found on the flats, are attracted by the sound made by a "popping cork". Cast your bait with a popping cork attached about 3 or 4 feet above the bait, and retrieve the bait by jerking the popping cork over the surface of the water making a distinctive popping sound. Pop the cork only once every two minutes at the most, so you don't scare the fish away.

Sharks (*all species*) are mostly caught drifting or slow trolling with live baits, or with bloody baits. While most authorities consider some sharks sportfish, most are easy to catch, and not very good fighters. Some shark meat is found on the tables of trendy restaurants, but, unless treated with unusual care when caught, it can be strongly flavored. Unless you have a need for the meat, don't destroy these fine creatures. Release them alive after they have been brought to the boat.

Snappers are all excellent eating. The deep water snappers, **red snapper** (*Lutjanus campechanus*) and **silk snapper** (*Lutjanus vivanus*) are caught in water 200 to 800 feet deep. The **cubera snapper** (*Lutjanus cyanopterus*), **vermilion snapper** (*Rhomboplites aurorubens*) and the **yellowtail snapper** (*Ocyurus chrysurus*) are found in depths of 60 to 200 feet. **Lane snapper** (*Lutjanus synagris*) are found in depths of 30 to 100 feet. **Mangrove snapper** (*Lutjanus griseus*) and **mutton snapper** (*Lutjanus analis*) prefer bays, creeks and mangrove sloughs. The offshore snapper are caught bottom fishing with shrimp or cut bait, or very slow deep trolling. The mangrove and mutton snappers are caught casting with shrimp or tipped jigs bounced off the bottom.

Snook (*Centropomus undecimalis*). Casting lures or large shrimp and retrieving the lure by slowly bouncing the lure over the bottom is a good technique for snook. Most snook fishing is done at night near bridges, lighted piers, or canals. Try to fish so your lures are retrieved through the edge of the halo of light. If you choose to drift your bait down to the edge of the halo you must be positioned so the tide carries your bait down tide to the halo. The start of the outgoing tide is a good time to fish. Both tarpon and snook prefer the change of the tide coupled with the change of light.

Spanish mackerel (*Scomberomorus maculatus*) are found in open water and in tidal flows. They can be caught by trolling, casting and drifting. Most fish are caught within two miles of the beach or in tidal inlets. Preferred baits include cut bait, spoons and jigs.

Striped Bass (*Morone saxialis*) are found in rivers, estuaries and the ocean over any type of bottom. Fishing methods include casting from shore, trolling and jigging from boats. They will take a wide variety of

Swordfish are a pelagic migratory species that are found in temperate and tropical waters from the surface to depths of 400-500 fathoms or more.

live or dead baits, pork rinds, bucktails, plugs, jigs, spoons, feathers, imitation worms.

Swordfish *(Xiphias gladius)* are an unfortunate example of the effects of overfishing. This fine-tasting fish was once fairly abundant but is now scarce. Most are caught by drifting whole squid, Spanish mackerel, or large mullet at depths of up to 400 feet. The fishing is generally at night 15 to 45 miles off shore.

Tarpon *(Megalops atlanticus).* The best place for catching tarpon is in the ocean inlets (called cuts). You can cast for them or drift live baits. The live baits can be very large shrimp, or any live fish. If you drift live fish, keep the baits at the surface. Most use tackle of 10 to 20 pound test, however fish to 120 pounds are now being taken by expert fly fishermen on as little as 4 pound-test class line. Tarpon also take a spoon with yellow feather trolled during the start of the outgoing tide.

Tripletail *(Lobotes surinamensis)* are found around buoys, markers and debris. After you see them, cast an artificial lure just past the buoy and retrieve slightly erratically.

Tunas, including **blackfin** *(Thunnus atlanticus),* **little tuna** *(Euthynnus alletteratus),* also called **bonito** or **false albacore,** and **skipjack** *(Katsuwonus pelamis)* are mostly caught casting after a school has been spotted. Preferred baits are artificial lures, including

Tuna are pelagic and migratory fish that travel in groups varying from three or four fish to schools of many thousands.

plugs, spoons and jigs. You can also pick up blackfin or bonito while trolling for kingfish or sailfish. The baits may be more effective tipped with a piece of cut bait. The bonito or little tuna is highly regarded as a fine food fish by Europeans and South Americans. It has light colored flesh.

Yellowfin tuna *(Thunnus albacares)* are also called **Allison tuna.** They are prized both as gamefish and table fare. Most are caught well offshore and generally run in large schools. The preferred method is trolling with whole dead baits, strip baits or sometimes they will even take artificial lures.

Wahoo *(Acanthocybium solanderi)* can be caught trolling, or casting at or near buoys or markers, or if you find one, under whales.

White marlin *(Tetrapturus albidus)* will be caught trolling, drift fishing with live bait, and kite fishing. For the kite technique see the notes on sailfish.

Index